Praise for *A Map of M*

T0024799

"In *A Map of My Want*, Faylita Hicks confronts the 'violence—the murdered women' and intergenerational trauma to reclaim the 'absolute right to my sex, / the absolute right to my life.' These haunting poems trace a journey from oppression and incarceration to hard-earned liberation and self-love. With searing honesty, Hicks declares, 'I bow before my many names' as she explores the complexities of identity, faith, desire, and the 'long flood / risking it all.' Through vivid details and musical language, Hicks conjures a 'vortex / in the static' where the political and personal collide. The collection builds to the triumphant manifesto, 'A Liberation All My Own,' a rallying cry for 'The access to myself unencumbered / by the insecurity of a shelter-less road' and 'To experience a liberation / all my own.' This is an essential collection that burns with resilience, eroticism, and the pursuit of freedom on every page."

—**RUBEN QUESADA**, author and award-winning editor of
Latinx Poetics: Essays on the Art of Poetry

"*A Map of My Want* is a triumph of the erotic. It's a poetic knowing of jail, sleeping cots, bills, and of riding feral pleasures beyond to the self's heat. Hicks' poetry is a wilful shake of the body, heart, and mind. 'Gawd forgive me. I loved a womxn / in a LaQuinta Inn. Showed her what it was like to be / worshiped, then I woke early and left before the alarm rang.' Their poetry sings. Invites the reader to sing along—ecstatically."

—**MAUD LAVIN**, author of *Push Comes to Shove*

"This collection reminds us that the truest representation of emotional truth is best derived through the fantastic. Each poem is a special magic that inhabits the deepest parts of the psyche, digs in, and resists forgetting."

—**AIREA D. MATTHEWS**, author of *Bread and Circus*

"*A Map of My Want* vividly paints a theology of self love, one that transcends the shifting world around it, and somehow anchors us, firm-footed, in the wanderlust of belonging. At times erotic, revealing, and steeped in the dangers of Americana, this collection eloquently ponders the journey we often overlook for the focus of some promised arrival."

—**DEBORAH MOUTON**, author of *Black Chameleon*

"Reading *A Map of My Want*, so muscular, impassioned, and wide-awake, it's not difficult to believe that bull's-eye poetry is alchemy, that healing the un-nursed self is healing the world. Faylita Hicks celebrates, with thunder and unshakable candor, her own hard-won erotic acumen and resilience."

—**CYRUS CASSELLS**, author of *Is There Room for Another Horse on Your Horse Ranch?*

"Few books have made me study the body as closely as Faylita Hicks' *A Map of My Want*, and how could I not when these poems insist that the body is something that can be 'Velcroed' to the self or others? This detachment of the body makes room for the speaker's meticulous observation of it. It multiplies and magnifies the body's already monstrous need for the erotic, the platonic, every kind of touch that exists pressurized into one hot gem. Too often we are fooled into thinking we are in control of our desires—Hicks has been gracious in the correction of our folly, in reminding us that the body always draws the map, and we merely follow it."

—**TAYLOR BYAS**, author of *I Done Clicked My Heels Three Times*

A
MAP
OF MY
Want

FAYLITA HICKS

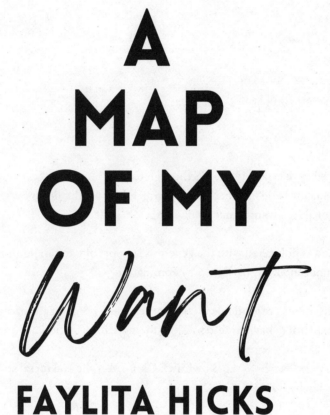

Haymarket Books
Chicago, Illinois

© 2024 Faylita Hicks

Published in 2024 by
Haymarket Books
P.O. Box 180165
Chicago, IL 60618
773-583-7884
www.haymarketbooks.org
info@haymarketbooks.org

ISBN: 979-8-88890-097-0

Distributed to the trade in the US through Consortium Book Sales and Distribution
(www.cbsd.com) and internationally through Ingram Publisher Services
International (www.ingramcontent.com).

This book was published with the generous support of Lannan Foundation, Wallace
Action Fund, and Marguerite Casey Foundation.

Special discounts are available for bulk purchases by organizations and institutions.
Please email info@haymarketbooks.org for more information.

Cover artwork "Roshi" © 2018 by Dawn Okoro. Acrylic and metal spikes on canvas.
Cover design by Rachel Cohen.

Printed in Canada by union labor.

Library of Congress Cataloging-in-Publication data is available.

10 9 8 7 6 5 4 3 2 1

For every version of me that has known great love and loss—and still managed to reclaim my dignity.

CONTENTS

THE PURSUIT

"The dichotomy between the spiritual and the political is also false, resulting from an incomplete attention to our erotic knowledge. For the bridge which connects them is formed by the erotic—the sensual—those physical, emotional, and psychic expressions of what is deepest and strongest and richest within each of us, being shared: the passions of love, in its deepest meanings."

—Audre Lorde, from "Uses of the Erotic: The Erotic as Power"

COASTING

Carlsbad Beach, CA | March 2022

Out of habit, I search the shore
for bodies. Black birds that dive
dead into the restless waves
to re-emerge incandescent
from feather to bone, a murmur
subtly surrendering to its thirst.

Out of habit, I sink into the beach's
bleached lip, gather my memories:
the wind's salt catching on the bridge of my tongue,
the trickle of laughter floating down the sighing coast,
the frothy bloom of a coastal morning stitching
            precious seconds between my toes.

Out of habit, my sister stares
into the wet fissure praying at our feet,
says *I don't want you to leave*
Escondido. I don't want to leave
California. But lately, I've been lying
awake on the cot in our mother's kitchenette,

counting—for hours—the birds.

Out of habit, I navigate the gossamer
of the year our brother died and our sister faded,
the year our young grew past their promise
and into the next iteration of us, the year
I buried my wonder under a pile of contracts
and calendars, the year I fed myself to the grasslands

coasting from one fatal moment to the next.

Out of habit, I close my eyes
and the Pacific's docile waves transform
into a relentless ebb of etches
in the small clock choking my wrist,
knowing that if I stay in the here and now,
I may never find my way back to the beginning.

Out of habit, my sister asks
why are you in a hurry to disappear.
Truly, I am in no hurry to appear
anywhere but here, at the end
of the world as we've known it:
our little lives—shining precursors

to the tide.

Out of habit, I swallow the horizon
racing towards us whole; think
what a wonder it must be to not know
the burden of time. What a gift it is
to not live, always, in between here or there;
to not be overcome with the limitlessness

of *need.*

ALCHEMY

"Everything, including time, changes in revolutionary time, and the clocks inherited from the old regime are usually too slow or too fast. A real revolution introduces a new time and space and a new relation to both time and space."

—Lerone Bennett Jr., from "Of Time, Space, and Revolution"

STEEL HORSES

Compton's bois rush their two-wheeled mares by the passenger
window my momma keeps pointing out of. Hiking they front wheels up
off the ground, they lean their heavy backs into the hard river
of the block, coaxing gravity to knock or not knock them down.
They roar and skirt through the bloody light on the backs of stallions
coated in syrupy bows of rain—toxic lime and anarchy's mandarin—
engine colors slick against the fading fair of all this Century Street grim.
My momma points out our hood, notes where I was almost buried
under the sick gremlin-green porches of the ghetto. Points out the corner
on which my daddy made her my momma and drives silently towards
our block and the pictures of her as a girl—the ones I never bothered
remembering. Reaching back for the last connection between us, she
points out the highlights for me to remember: Where she knew he
was man, where she knew she wasn't, where she first knew love
as a weapon. I am only half-listening, watching the Black boi
next to us jerk they wheels up into the air, their grill angry
in the West Coast burn. I can barely hear her I am so busy
wondering if I am somewhere they are going, what it feels like
to have all that heavy in between my legs. *What if
I was heavy between the legs?* What would it feel like
to hang my body from a machine—to feel the trickle of time
gaining mass between my skin and shift? My momma stops
the car, turns at the intersection saying, *This is the farthest I've ever gone.*
And I turn to the rearview just in time to watch the bois in the mirror
explode past Century and disappear into the horizon beyond.

ON BECOMING A BRIDGE FOR THE BINARY

In the desert, who I was evaporates in the belly of a long night.
    Makes it difficult to know exactly when I become a valley: a facility of ghosts

    starved for the heated flicks, the mouth of someone else's suns. Sxns
with my mother's chin. Some with my father's knuckles. Some with matted fur

curving the spoon of their backs. Some with hook-shaped cocks.
    Some with escozul for throats that glow in the after-sun, after me.

In the desert, I am a task of breath. A bridge of flesh and brine,
    turning back to watch everything in California burn. A flex of womxn

    I patrol the lip of a country tired of my mud-caked face, hover
over the trail of my own salt and demise, travel south//southwest

listening to the horns of Los Angeles bleed into the expanse,
    the city's lights trickling off along the smooth glassy back of the interstate.

        I slide between Los Angeles and my first death. Bury myself
        in the Chihuahuan's hunger—a kind of sorrow

        sweating blades of bromegrass,
        sleeping in puddles of hushing grama,

        my legs dangling from a bed
        of dehydrated moons.

        Who we are now—a river of hands
        fishing ourselves up from out of the dirt.

        Who we are now—tired game
        wandering//borderless.

        We ride between Los Angeles and our second death. A desert of flesh
        drowning in the Chihuahuan's thirst—a canvass

marked through by incessant light,
we are a host of fresh leather

cut from the cracked earth's fringe; our wrists a weary flag
for weather to chew through.

In the desert, who I was breaches the belly of this disruptive night.
Who I am now—a kind of boi traveling south//southwest: as far as the stars will
take me

into the land coughing up all of my names, the skin of the road warm
against the bottoms of my blackened feet turned grey from hunting an exit//ocular.

My scars, a scattering of messages about the end. What I am now—hurled
through the red enchanted, soft and affected. Makes it easy to know

the strategy of every border: to drape a gold chain around my dark and heavy
waist and pull.

In the desert, who I was is buried somewhere
in this pale state's   eviscerated edge.

CHIRON'S BREACH

"In astrology, Chiron symbolizes the 'wounded healer' in we mere mortals."

—Aliza Kelly, from "Chiron Is the Therapist of the Cosmos," *The Cut*

I gather and gather myself. Prepare for a turning
    of the page on which I am the scythe-like beak of an ibis,

a blooming lily amongst too many blood-thirsty thorns,
    a whale slamming through wall after wall of water

out into the weapons of this world;
    fall deep into the crevasse of Sedona's flora.

Clusters of canopy shiver with my arrival,
    their pale limbs cold and bare

in the ceaseless blaze of headlights at twilight.
    A concert of mechanical hungers aching

for the dirt of the desert's nakedness, refracted light snakes
    seductively through the shadows

cast by us avid voyeurs. Like me, others had come
    into the rifts of Arizona to tour a siloed wildness,

lie down their heads and posture. Find god and fuse
    with the incalculable throb of currents

tied taut and thin under this ancient nation's thirsty soil
    and punishing sun. From the Pacific's

waterlogged missive, I had come in search of an Origin.
    More than my ichor, I needed to know the particular conjure

of my structure, the bawdy shape of my passions inherited
    from time's incline. I wanted

to convince myself of an affinity
    for healing—an aptitude for kinetic evolution.

Like the planet itself, an orgasmic creature floating
    through the edgeless sea of the universe—

I needed to know I could, again, be thoroughly alive.
    Even after a cataclysmic series of disasters.

Around and around Bell Rock, I hiked until I saw twisted juniper
    with all its pulsing and braided branch,

all the satisfactions of an organic wax and wane.
    Staring out into this abyss of bush I counted

millions of solar flares, each of them fingering
    the ultraviolet of evening, a tinted mimosa

pressing its silk mouth to my swollen knees.
    Exhausted, I stopped to appreciate the horizon's massage,

the tantric hum of its *viva magenta*; a shade of praise
    for this breach of light, this long-awaited infiltration.

From this fervent shore, back into the abyss of my America
    I tripped, teasing an undulating map

tugging at me until I threatened deluge, until
    within me, a floor trembled

with the harbinger of the end of my era—a long flood
    risking it all—from sea to shining sea.

I continued to fall, to slide into the congested heart
    of the hill country, the green stucco and arid patches of my San Marcos.

Sewing pieces of myself beneath the Guadalupe River,
    I went down into the rice grasses, finally

in fealty to the mud of my blood, the rich silence
    of my many dark deaths inherited

seeping through the partially reclaimed
    dirts of Texas.

My mirror, a diamond rattle slipping easily through the skin
    of every new radical movement against my life,

my every uprising, treated like a venom seeking inoculation.
    And still I crawl, one wheel in front of the other

to the beat of
    a cacophonous wave.

USES OF THE EROTIC: SHIFTING TIMELINES

"Within the celebration of the erotic in all our endeavors, my work becomes a conscious decision—a longed for bed which I enter gratefully and from which I rise up empowered."

—Audre Lorde, from "Uses of the Erotic: The Erotic as Power"

I feel the water before the water reaches me—a mirror
of my own urgency slipping past the bank, the curb,
and into each of the cars in the lot. I've done all I can
to prepare, but every street in this rural city fills
with the rush of the Guadalupe River's muck and mire.
Someone is going to drown tonight. To soothe myself,
I trudge through the flood, head back to my apartment
on the first floor, a step up from the place with no fire alarm,
and a step down from the college dorms. Dripping, I pet
the cat, then the dog, grab the leftover Barefoot wine, and fuck me.
It is the screaming laughter of the neighbors running
in their flip-flops to their doors on other floors,
the crackling sky flipping switches of light across
my living room's yellowed stucco, the pounding chords
of the monsoon positioning itself right over the lip of my porch,
and the milky slip of the evening's sun peaking through
the cloud's erratic smoke that makes me flare violently
on the couch. Resting, I find some primitive comfort
in the knowledge that at least, this time, I chose
to die naked, wet, and pleasantly exhausted.

LIFE

"The spirit of the ancestors (the dead) and the spirits of the living
are connected, and it is the responsibility of the living to ensure
that the dead are given honor, praise, and constant recognition . . .
The two worlds are as mountains mirrored in a pool of water . . ."

—Corey C. Stayton, from *The Kongo Cosmogram:
A Theory in African-American Literature*

BEFORE MY BAPTISM, A FUNERAL

Jaded, the lake I was to be given to
was full of those partially drowned

canoes, their plastic paddles
languishing in the moss-ridden waters,

each shuddering against the caress
of my small and curious hands

as I washed away the pine and stick
of my first dead.

After Bible study, I'd rushed towards
the chirping in the brush and the creaking deck

of the lake house, looking for the verse
I'd need before I fell into bed,

but found there in the dirt path at dusk
a body purpled black: a Great-Tailed Grackle

lying still. A warning of grief's desired familiarity
—just outside my cabin's window.

I knew, even then, that for this I had prayed,
all of every day, until long after all the frogs had gone,

until there were no more distant suns
left to crawl across the ribboned sky and windless field.

I had prayed until my spirit hummed with the fired-up degrees
of my last adolescent summer to know

the shape and name of my life's purpose:
to know the greatest and the least of us—and love.

THE ORIGIN OF MY DESIRE

At seventeen, I perched in the green threshold of my mother's house, the omen of an eclipse. Her obscure promise of death, the consequence of life, I lingered hollow above the intimate violence of my parent's love, was left with only the vestige of a voice, a mere echo of myself. A glimmer of their once erect soul–their ancestral octaves–I was arrested in the bridge of their bodies. A promise of alignment, I tightly grasped the rust-speckled frame of our front door, a design of two edges once confirmed connected. I, their child, a vintage veil of an always or a forever, left to dream. In the liminal, I surged with the knowing of what would be lost if I fell through too soon. But still too young for any coherent sagacity, my aqueous flames refused to hush. A turquoise incineration, my desire to live pooled in the globe of my waist—dangled soft as knives, from the summit of my sacral, danced from my candied earlobes.

I decided then to let my unborn slip through the brim of my hips, unevolved. I knew far too much to give into the call of that tide. I would let each latent child leak from me a giggling hex code, a glowing spectrum spiraling about me; through and out and into the world because I was, and still am, freshly obsessed with the fecundity of my own light, the potential of my own shadow to become:

a snow-tipped mountain gyrating
    glacially and alone to the jazz of evolution
        off in the distance—a lover unto itself;

    the glass shine of a red wheelbarrow
        hung from Walmart's rafters above the heads
           of Williams's impatient patrons;

a dry, cheddar-crusted fish
    fluttering in the grip of a toddler's pink palm,
        air sucked and already gutted;

    the thin wax pastel of every church's sacraments accompanied by
        a bitter plum cleanse and a half-hearted prayer
           to canonized cannibals, thanking them for the stain;

an emerald rainforest dripping eternally into the coral
    and corrugated sands of our many, many-tongued
        cerulean-licked rivers;

    several prickly pears purpled black, circling the feet of sage saguaros
        with their arms stretched out to fit the fat-bellied indigo azure
            sitting so large and still on their peppered faces;

a mouth aching for color,
    hxr tongue tracing the svelte outlines
        of a buttery mango swollen ripe;

    splitting wetly, a fat berry
        bleeding ruddy in the puncture;

the iron rails of a slated cathedral
    teetering reckless over
        the emulsified gunmetal of my streets;

    the tanned clay of castles
        dressed in the rough silk
            of fire-necked plateaus;

the sticky paste of L'Absolu Rouge
    caressing hxr partitioned mouth;

    the perpetual student
        canvassing the ever-wild
           of all known universes.

And still I perch in the threshold of my watery house, an ever-lingering omen, an ordained deluge—throbbing.

FINGER HUT

Knuckle deep, I am quietly unzipped
beneath Netflix and therapy sessions,
wrestling the wet silence of myself.   I am going
numb with repentance. How quickly
need feeds into my cold hands—
like syrup. In the dark I forget
who I was before the feral moan
of silicone and Doxepin. I drag
my fingers through my curtains,
panting to the memory of the last time
I was touched by something
other than synthetic light.
Growl beneath the glowing screens,
all fang and grunt, turn in the dirt, rest.
In the shower afterwards, I say
to myself *Congratulations.*
Your limits have increased.
Turn the dial all the way up
and wait for the heat to find me.

#LOVEMACHINE

I say "my body loves their body" and the editor corrects me
"the word 'body' is dehumanizing" and of course

the editor is correct—that a body is not the same as a person
but I wasn't talking about people. I was

talking about the body I arrived to the afterparty in—
the one Velcroed to my person, trying to Velcro to other persons.

I say "my body leaks when it sees their body" and the professor
gets hard around the mouth at my obsession with fluids and bodies,

says "there is nothing new here" and of course
the professor is correct—that there is nothing new.

I like all of my things worn in—
except for my technology, which is always

refreshing itself. I type "mybodyisbreakingdown"
and streaks of red

dance under my stitched words,
making me stroke

the small body of my machine
and cradle it like a bird, apologizing.

Inside it, smaller apologies
cradling smaller birds,

stroking. Inside of them,
bodies invisible as birds.

FOREIGN BODIES

"Over the next 30 years, 143 million people are likely to be uprooted by rising seas,
drought, searing temperatures, and other climate catastrophes."
—UN Intergovernmental Panel on Climate Change 2022 report

You cannot tell me
there is nothing wrong

with the weather.
Scientists discovered

a new species of blind
"flesh-toned" fish

flushed out from a hole
in the earth of Kurdistan

almost an exact year after
a photographer discovered

the pronate body of Alan Kurdi
flushed out from a hole

in the earth of Turkey
almost four years before

a journalist discovered
the pronate bodies of Óscar Ramirez

and Angie Valeria
flushed out from a hole

in the earth of Texas
this past Sunday.

The origins of this
new species of fish

are: widely speculated,
essentially unknown

but it is clear—they are
proliferating underground.

You cannot tell me there is nothing
wrong:

I digested this data and disintegrated
on a molecular level—

am now an ironic history of black heat
coaxing out your air and tearing through

your defined shape. I have become
the hidden hyphen

strangling the ice of your hips
and shredding. There is something wrong

with the weather—with my mouth—
a silhouette of mud.

I've swallowed mxn for millennia am now
a register of cyclical genders, flushing out sex

from a queer hole in my body. To say I am unknown
is to say I am in flux—sucking on all the names

and waterlogged roots dissoluble
in the hinge of my *blackblue* skin;

both vessel and vision—I have become
a fish

and a womxn and ready to die—
a hurricane in the heart. My species survives,

our wilted crowns bent at the center
as green wave after green wave

swaddles itself around our necks
to bruise deep and distinctive. Listen to us

bubble up and scratch our heads
against the open air. Whistle and arc.

Awash along the thinning coast are our bodies,
once lost in the sway of the ocean,

are ribbon along the white shore of this man's land.
A flush of color—we have always been

going or coming with the tide.
You cannot tell me—there is nothing wrong

with the weather. I can feel it in my jaw—
the thirst for copper-tinged sediment and meat

fresh from the dying fields. Can't you feel it?
California can't stop shaking. What it knows

runs back and forth beneath the surface:
a beast of ruin gnawing on our dead;

the fires of Paradise chew
through the face of the state,

smoke out the menagerie of darkened bodies
that clog its anxious streets with gangs of *amen*

to camp on the floor of this wild. Can't you feel it?
Greenland is melting. The yellow milk

swished from its mouth—out into the ocean—
is enough to feed the world's hungry

with salt and suspended silt. When you turn
from yourselves to see your cities burning—

do you not melt? Am I the only one on fire?
Texas is drowning. The flooded borders

overcome with waves of *helpushelpushelpus*
congeal into cement puddles large enough to float

and swallow our country of survivors. Are we not
now—all wet? Is my body the only one still gasping for air?

You cannot tell me—there is nothing
wrong with the weather.

THINGS I DO IN A STORM

"Almost all of Texas was without power for four days after a frigid winter storm,
named Uri."

—Paul Alexander, from "Greg Abbott's Failures Mean Texas Could Suffer Another
Freezing Winter Blackout," *The Bulwark*

i.
Crawl back into the cocoon of myself
a pile of laundry covering my fragile furless body
in the choking scent of Tide, a wave masking me
from the spindly legs of the chill that finally came—
had been oncoming   for decades.

ii.
Step outside to smoke, draw in the air
what I imagine were the worried faces
of my father and his new wife and their new child—
watching the flurry grow
from the leather couch in the living room
in the heart of the cold, tiny house
that once was to be ours.
I knew my father wouldn't be thinking
about the house or the leather, but about the land
and his dogs scattered on it. His faithful
left to weather the unlikely   on their own.

iii.
Listen to the river city of San Marcos unplugged.
Look over the fields flooded with snow. Strain
for any sounds of crying or calls for help.
Wonder about the snow of Texas reaching:
Florida. Arizona. California.
Send my smoke to dangle
over the trees in Santa Fe's Escondido.

iv.
Charge all of my machines, my digital diaries
fixed with tinseled confessions;
unhook from the world, ask
The Nothing Left: *what now?*
Be greeted with the kind of silence
only death or snow can offer.
Hold my cell phone up to the sky,   pray for a signal.

v.
Read only the books with red covers, the warmth
an illusion to convince me that I am alive
in the world, a part of the words constructing the worlds
where streets are filled with strangers
making memories or mistakes,
where I am sitting on a rooftop in Colombia or
catching a taxi in Manhattan or making sweaty love
on silk sheets in Shanghai. So hot,
so sticky, my body keeps

                    shining through the night.

vi.
Consider Joan Didion's potential futures in California
as opposed to my potential futures in California.

vii.
Remember that forty miles
from the border of Mexico   my mother says my sister is
sleeping on the pavement
outside of a laundromat or a coffee house—
and no one can wake her now.

The second youngest of us four,
she was the first to give birth
as I, the eldest, refused. For her, I send
the smoke instead of the snow

because one will take her from us
faster than the other.

viii.
Paint my fingers and mouth red
for the first time in over a year.
Kill the Hennessy. Kill the Bacardi.
Kill the Malibu, too.

ix.
Decide not to apologize to my father
about blocking his calls. Decide not to
stay in the river city when this is over. Decide
not to blame myself for my sister's   bad weather.
Decide not to keep the biscuits
in the microwave. Decide not to watch
the movies I downloaded. Decide not to turn
off the faucet. Compared to him,
keeping my pipes from freezing
is all I know how to do.

x.
Crawl back into the cocoon of myself.

GAWD FORGIVE ME

I paid the rent today. The lights are still on.
The water still runs. I bought groceries—again.
I put $20 in the tank and $20 on the dresser.
I bought a dress, a black lace slip that clings.
Through the fabric, I felt myself and fantasized
about womxn with meaty palms, fingers wrapped
around my throat. I came several times today.
Forgive me, I bought shoes. A pair for every day
I meant to go out and be seen/carefree/wasted.
A pair for every day I meant to be something, anything.
I didn't pray over the bodies of the broken this morning.
Instead, I had coffee from Starbucks. I drank a half-bottle
of Knob Creek, a half-bottle of Turkey. Forgive me.
I bought a box of cigars and I threw them away. I donated
nothing this year. Gawd, forgive me. I loved a womxn
in a La Quinta Inn. Showed her what it was like to be
worshiped, then I woke early and left before the alarm rang.
Dear Gawd, I ate cheese from 7-Eleven. I had a Four Loco.
I bought a pair of sunglasses. Watched anime until four am.
Lay in bed for hours, watching the fan on my ceiling whip
around and around and around and around and around—
said nothing. Wrote nothing. Went nowhere. Gawd, forgive me.
I did nothing today. I went down for water, thought nothing
about the refugees. Thought nothing about cancer. Forgot
the name of my dead husband. Gawd, forgive me.
I forgot his name today.

MY LOVER WANTS TO KNOW WHERE I AM

If I am in Albuquerque, it is to borrow
time as a reclaimed silhouette of womxn
singing in my lover's entryway—a cloud,
heavy over the headboards. *Look I am here
now.* An ache gyrating through the artist's studio
in Houston, jerking on a bear-backed rug, my fat
breasts in my lover's hands like wet bowls of feathers.
What smokes more than this? I ask while in Denver,
my hips swung around the broken faucet
of my lover's neck, cradling the strange
howls crawling out of us. My fingers,
little spiders climbing out from tight drains
ask: *Is it memory, the terror of touch?* I myself,
a sliding scale of *do not* or *but softly*, went back
to Baltimore—with its cocoa butter and warm showers
and flexed heels—looking for an answer. I went back
to El Paso for its back seats and seasoned bone marrow
and unprotected borders. I went back to Columbus
for its butter and cream and I never left Los Angeles,
though I said I would. I went back to Chicago, though I said I wouldn't,
looking for my panties and my moisturizer and my last layer of skin.
I never left Killeen—with its pump and grunt—though I said I would
and I know this is a problem but the truth is, sometimes I like the discipline.
My lover wants to know where I keep going when I close my eyes. I say
*I am in Portland—pray for me. I am in Vegas—do not call.
I am in New York. Please—come get me.*

BONFIRE BRIDES

"The embers of a Thousand Years / Uncovered by the Hand / That fondled them
when they were Fire / Will stir and understand— "

—Emily Dickinson, from "1383"

Remember when we hurried
        ourselves into the evening's sacral blaze:
Our coal-covered bridal gowns
        drenched in the long silver

of our mother's years? Our hearts ceaselessly
        sucking on their stars, long dead?
Our laughter pouring out
        like a sacrifice to age and weather?

If we had known what lay beyond the gates
        of our hooded child, would we have even left?
Would we have so happily run out into the enflamed morning
        with our fists and queries and hunger? Should we have stayed?

Lover, do you remember when we wanted god?
        Were all tendril? Sweet-cheeked for heaven?
Do you remember when we were sick with Bible verses and hymns?
        Our mouths overcome with hallelujah?

Our mouths slowly sewn into the crooked neck
        of every sunset? Do you remember the place
where we laid down our child-shapes
        and grew out our hair?

Yours—an unrelenting wave slipped from the bed
        of your precious scalp
down into the looped bone
        of your back?

Mine—a cacophony of glitter and grease leaping
     from the barrel of my hungry scalp
to arrive restlessly
     around the pillars of my ears?

Do you remember the place where we skipped—
     two gxrls chasing themselves
across the lake's green and warm lid
     off into the untested fields

of prairie grass and unchecked verbena?
     The place, remember, where we learned
the dissonant lean of every foot worn
     into the unpaved pathways?

Somewhere outside of Dallas—
     where we skinned our knees
running after pink-fisted kisses
     from suns who, back then, hung a praise

before our names? Where I buried my first dead—
     a bird I found at the lake house?
Where we swore to never be like our mothers
     or our fathers?

Where we swore, under god's morning light,
     to be more like the persevering comets
falling well-worn yet joyous into our cabins, night after night?
     Do you remember where, together, we came

from a yard full of Jesus? Where he was
     under every wooden plank, every split stone—
always guaranteed
     to follow us home?

Jesus—we thought we'd have more time.
     Jesus—what happened to time?

I blinked and we were in love—
      then out of love—

then child-shaped again—then not.
      Then the both of us alone. Together.
The both of us crying into the empty
      of our kitchen sinks.

Jesus—how did we
      get here, again?

MY GIRLFRIEND WANTS ME TO SAVE HER FROM HER MARRIAGE

She is waiting
     for me to let her in   unable to

make the love herself
     without tearing her self apart.

She wraps her fingers around my waist and wishes

that she were a minnow
     instead of a forest.

It's easier to be
     lost in the rush of our siloed current

than to be known
     by the full reach   of her husband's machete.

She begs to be
     undone—quickly.

But I know his machete
     is not what she means.

She wraps her fingers around my wrists and pours

into me
     her self:

a cast of shadows
     lipping the desiccated opening

of my first mouth.
     Her *please-don't-leaves*

an orphaned technology
     in the bridge of my throat,

olive branches she has hidden
     like small weapons in the fat rice of my back teeth.

She is my cavity—
     an argument I will never stop having.

THE SKYBRIDGE IN THEIR DIVORCE

My mother points to the tiles on the floor
facing the slow yawn of sliding doors
at the entry of Gardena Hospital's infinite
wound—opening. Closing. Opening.
Whistles *Here is where you were born
and almost weren't*. I lick at the spot,
cooing to myself *It's alright. It's alright.
You're going to be fine.*

I am fine—the first year
a series of Greyhound buses pull
me by my umbilical cord from her lap,
tug at me like a leather conduit

tethered to a plane with a photo of
my father's feathering face on its helm;
their love—another casket
on its way to the Gulf War.

For a while, I am fine. I am fine
before my father gouges Iraq out of Kuwait,
the sand out of the 1990s; before my father begins
to sleepwalk through the rocky hills,

his face slick with the syndrome, a haunting
as wide and black as the streets
of the decommissioned veteran graveyard
known as Copperas Cove, Texas;

before my father becomes a chronic disorder
of dreams deferred; before his chest becomes
unable to lock onto air long enough
to keep him breathing while he sleeps,

becomes a battered flag hanging just above half-mast;
before my father gathers together our aging love,
devouring canteen after canteen
of our family's only artillery left—our time

—I am fine. I am fine for years

before my mother begins to lose her teeth
to the slow erosion of her faith in kin, a curse
from the ever wild of California's South Central,
a scattering of close calls and instinctual surrendering;

before my mother is domesticated and pretty
for church on Sundays; before my mother becomes
one-half of a new stranger shouting in my house;
before the under hours of my childhood turn

into nightmares; before I am no longer a child
but a sister-wife, a second mother
translating grief for my sisters, her half-borns;
before my mother buries her hard-earned wisdoms

underneath the light of a god
with a gift for murder;
before I am drowned
and reborn in this god's name.

I am fine. I am fine for years—

the ones that come to me, still,
hour after hour sneaking through security,
sniffing through my bags, protesting
any and every apostrophe, rusted rails

attached to empty brick-red seats,
their plastic shells tethered together

by the steel of my mother's lungs
unchecked in yet another airport terminal.

and I don't think this is fine—
but now I am always most at home
when I am coming home
—crossing. Uncrossing.

Crossing any distance
between them and now.
Now, I come attached
to the static bustle of escape.

I am a plastic disc of:
goodbye goodbye goodbye. For good.
Point me towards any exit that matters.
I will untangle my fat, buttery hands

from my father's anxious and slippery hands
and lean into the act of flying
as the first of my mother's
flowering clots to dip.

Only an etch of a sliding scale
—a dollop of acrylic intimacy—
I have hated having to hold on
to any of this: my empty hands;

the belt; the switch; the punishments
of my mother's child-shaped punishments;
the annual itinerary of our home's insecure seasons;

the irreverent split
of my uplifted chest, sharpened by age
and parentless dissonance; this growing Black mist of mine;
my now indisputable destiny as pain's center;
my mother, my father, and their children.

It has been tiring coming back to myself again.
Again. Whenever I'm picking up at the airport now,
I hold up a fence. Or the electric tandem
of my queer technicolor heritage.

I hold up my conditioned love
to protect myself from their vintage egos.
I hold up the good bustle and air. For them
I've held still—in the air—for decades.

Even so, my mother points to herself
lying still on a cheap beige carpet
in an old trailer in North Carolina,
like a mask of light or a casualty of gravity
or an abandoned conduit of air—
whistles *Here is the year I gunned down a man*
with a face full of feathers, a bed full of leather hides,
and instructions on how to not tether ourselves together.

And I'm fine. I'm fine. I'll be alright up here.

STRING THEORY

"String theory is an attempt to unite the two pillars of twentieth century physics—
quantum mechanics and Albert Einstein's theory of relativity—with an overarching
framework that can explain all of physical reality."

—Adam Mann, from "What Is String Theory," Live Science

My love—a pulsing gravity
pulling your body back down
to mine on the ground.

Do not be afraid.
I have had practice.
I know how to braid

myself together with others,
their names and faces
the wax-coated thread

keeping me from going
too far over the licking
ridge of Lake Michigan,

where I last refused
to surrender.
Your ill-advised exposure

to my reverberating kiss,
my thinly veiled promises
of answered questions,

is more so what you should fear.
There are no revelations
for you here. I am the ellipsis.

I perpetually contrast and expand,
casting wave after wave out across
the long and convoluted verse.

Rarely   am I giving
simple answers,
my love.

FAREWELL TO FLESH

> "Carnival, literally a 'farewell to flesh,' describes a period of turning outward that precedes a time of inward movement. The dynamic flux of equilibrium is upheld."
>
> —Louis Martinié and Sallie Ann Glassman, *The New Orleans Voodoo Tarot*

I crave the Carnival
of my dénouement
—the last festival
of my life—a silk tent
pulsating with the creatures
of my carnal infrastructure.
To be and not be
the silver hatchet, spilling
crude in my bed, performing
every little death
in the belligerent light
of an evening come
set too soon.
To float an array
of divans, teasing
the freshly slipped pelts
of my paramours
with the whelm
of my kinetic urgency,
an acrobat riding
their wheels—hot!
Always. I need to be
needed. I yearn endlessly
for the dimming delights
of my curated innocence,
the borderless potential
of my reign over
my whole being,
unchecked. Let me
confess. I can come

home anytime I want.
I choose not to come
home alone.

LIVING WILL AND TESTAMENT

When I am old and tired of being tired, when my spine is as thin as hair, my eyes opaque sheets cloudy with missing memories, when I can no longer hold myself close with my tiny, tiny bird hands, can no longer feel for myself the heavy dimple of my belly, when my feet lose meat and my hips blotch like ripe banana-skin—if it is time to: let me go. Let me go to the river to greet the green hall of my death with laughter and obscenity. Let me fall into bed one last ecstatic time, so I can surrender myself to the feather and thread, shade and shake of my pillows once more before the shades are drawn. I want my last dance to be with someone who reminds me of me, a vortex of a grin swallowing me whole with their worship of: my body, my mind, my spirit. I want my last kiss to blast into my mouth and live in the well of me, a single aurora vibrating until I slow and still. Let my last taste be salty and sweet, a silky morsel dissolving on my tongue. Let the last sound be the acoustics of guttural laughter, forbidden sex, raucous applause, a riot's chant, and a newborn crying. Give me the soft breeze of a midsummer afternoon gliding between my legs, the scent of an oncoming storm, the base drop, the shattering glass, the car horns, the fuzzy bee floating across the quiet floor. I want a wave lapping the back door of my home. Give me a home. I want one last look in the mirror, one last glance at the womxn I've become. And just before closing, give me one last shot at the bar. If I am loved at all, there will be rows and rows of wilting white roses, lavender and hyssop, spider lilies and Spanish moss, frayed palm leaves and fresh-cut grass; there will be bowls of milk and honey, cinnamon and gingerroot mixed with whiskey or rum, seawater and salt and hot peppers. If I am remembered at all, there will be a thick-waisted mxn, a stripper who makes six figures a year, and an ex-minister/trans-beauty to start off my eulogy. The last meal will be everything I've ever eaten. There will be creams and fresh-baked breads. Fish stuffed with peppers. Candy stones and balloons made out of sugar. If I am remembered at all, every person in attendance will fast for three days and three nights before coming to my funeral. Someone should come to my funeral. If not my child, then anyone standing outside the corner store will do. They should rest and someone should rent a room for resting because my funeral will last for seven days. For seven days, sweaty musicians should be unable to keep their hands from twitching over their instruments, unable to hold their liquor or their wails. Sing me to sunrise! There should be horrible poems being read late into the next morning. Over lukewarm coffee and gin, someone should quote Romans 8:38-39 and make the sign of Yemáya. Someone should fall in love at my funeral! *Please, let it end with love.* Let there be a day of giving! On this day, everyone should eat only what someone else has offered and can only receive when they have offered something. At the church, only womxn should lead the prayers. The prayers should be to my long-dead mother or my long-dead first husband or my long-dead second wife or my long-dead chastity. Someone should make fun of the prayers. The whole church should laugh. Let the church have windows as tall as the pillars, a garden that empties out into the street so that the people I never knew can come into the air conditioning and eat! Someone should be baptized in the nearby river, in a sudden fit of joy! They should be washed clean of their insecurities and doubt. Rise—new disciples of themselves! There should be a story, a new story, written about the old one that died. She should be dangerously fierce, Black, and hungry! She should be a he the second time around. He should be deliciously handsome, Black, and hungry! Surely someone will think they saw her once, walking around with her long-twisted pipe, him with his gold-dipped wreath of gloriosa, them with their ticking hips. On the seventh day, at the funeral for the living and the dead, I want to sit on the church's wall, sweaty in my best red velvet gown under which I am wearing nothing, watching my body burn—one last time.

THE WIDOW AND I

For W.H.

Tired of trying to be touched
in places that no longer exist,

we amuse ourselves in the dark
by hyphenating our names

with invisible bodies, smoking
menthols and laughing

about the large dicks
of our dead husbands.

We share tips about screwing
our tears down to the floorboards,

stowing away our carnalities
deep in the grips of arbitrary men

—sometimes women—erasing any evidence
we ever resisted the sanctuary of sleep.

Gyrating slow, we dip
our shoulders into the swelling Atlantic—

reach back for whatever can be recovered
from the flood.

She finds a conch shell. I find the cowrie. We count
the sand we've gathered in our bowls.

LIBERTY

"According to the traffic incident report from the March 10 stop, a cardboard sign on the back of [Korryn] Gaines's car read: 'Any Government official who compromises this pursuit to happiness and right to travel will be held criminally responsible and fined, as this is a natural right or freedom.'"

—Colin Campbell, *Baltimore Sun*, August 6, 2016

A GXRL'S TRIP HOME

We are almost there I tell the womxn,
clutching the car's agitated wheel, steering
us between the year and its mourning.

Two viscid stretches of lavender,
they petal and melt in the chase
of my palms—blooming in the backseat.

Flexing in endearing pose, they ride
the glide and release of every yearning
attached to our first few missed exits in Texas:

a first turn towards our buried or burned;
another turn towards our sickled bodies;
a third turn towards our terminal disease: love.

Once friends or lovers or both, we each held death
in the silhouette of our ribs, our many griefs
like blades of grass stretched out all around us.

But our triptych desire, novel as it was in its run
down the sweaty vertebrae of the highway to Galveston,
is now a tale of three once sea-filled bowls—

empty, overturned, and flat.
A parable about how

time gorges on memory,
weather has its way with the heart,
faith fails us all, sometimes.

Whoever we were when we left Austin
faded with the famine summer of our lives,
died of thirst out along the side of the road,

is left to the lengthening night.
No telling now who we will be
once we finally arrive wherever we are going.

We are almost there I try to tell the womxn
still clutching each other in the backseat and crying.
We are almost there. We are almost there.

Hold on. Please—hold on.

AFTER THE GEORGE FLOYD PROTESTS,
MY STRANGE DREAM

That first night, I fell asleep to the redolent
symphony of shouting, fireworks, and cracking glass.
The beatboxing of block after block
breaking into my rest, tickling my wrist.

Twitching, I dreamed a dream.

A strange dream in which my desires—
a clean and laughter-filled street, the absolute right to my sex,
the absolute right to my life—were met
with the swords of the warrior Ogun.

In the dream, the bedroom was whiplashed red,
chants flooding the halls, pulling me from my pleasure.
Crawling out from between the legs of a womxn
with my name still wetly slathered across hxr chin,

I cradled the lewd silk of our sweetened venom—
up against the hot swell of my caged chest, waded out
through the front door, into the murky billows
of the damned and the damnable,

marched up the street past the Autozoned and the Targeted
into the arrest of our uncivility—the arrest of our love—
a Black light of adoration thrown suddenly from
the branches of our capitol, my transfigured husk

a dying star set swinging

over the blooming crowd of lavender orchids: soft reconstructions
of my ungendered generation, shuddering beneath the red
of the rocket's permanent glare. Falling into a hungry field
of fertile sediment—where from all our womb-ones have come—

I drowned in the burn. Only in death
was I then allowed to name myself,
to lay down and rest as the sojourn
of this country's smoldering years.

THE REAL REASON WE CAN'T HOOK UP AGAIN TONIGHT

I could hold you in the soil
of my partitioned mouth;
a new earth carrying you
in this abandoned entryway.
A beginning, a root stretched beneath you,
like this. But still—
I have not learned
to hold my breath. Still—
I chew on whatever I'm given,
so stop giving me things. Mxn
have given me things before. You
have given me things before. A lick
of wood, like the hard-unforgiven
tongue of a slobbering street dog
with boxed ears, covered in cuts
and fleas and sniffing garbage.
Once—your rifle. A long hollow finger
aimed at the crowd of my body, aimed at the young
and pretty face of my gxrl
in search of meaning or a husband
with a fat handle; aimed at the young
and pretty face of my boi in search of
food or a wife with a deep gouge.
You a casket of fine weather,
having buried yourself into my back,
gave me a blade to swallow—a stench of metal
to press against my tilted neck.
I chewed and chewed and now it is begging
to come up out of me
as a shovel. A hard worm
tired of my many absences. You are coming
up out of me, a golem of time, messy
with my clay. I am begging you—
Stop giving me things to destroy.

51

BEFORE DUSK, SAY MAYBE

"The orange skies this morning are a result of wildfire smoke in the air. Strong winds over the past few days transported ash from fires in Northern California and the Sierra Nevada into the region."

—Tweet posted by Bay Area Air Quality (@AirDistrict), September 9, 2020

A crisis: How we came easily
    to the suckling winds of California,

how the slow climb from the madness
    of our dirt bed

became the defining feature of our affair,
    a searing headline stenciled in ash.

From me you came and to me you will return—
    our anatomies tethered together

in an occasional vigil to time,
    our combined temperatures writhing

on the floor of our young universe—
    so, my love, remember this:

There is no you without me.

I do not enjoy this ache, the depth of it. Once, your love
    —an eclipse of feverish sky—

slid into me, between my shades
    as a thrust of tangerine wine

dabbing my walls in eternal eve;
    a concentrated scatter of intense horizon.

It rang   violently in the untouched   places
   —the sodomized cities of me—

where I wanted to be moaned into, your aubade
    touching me   neon.

But now my love
    you are too invasive. A parasite

taking my entire orgasm
    as your own. Stealing

away my evergreen gasps,
    my evergreen spread of garden.

Between my legs
    —the salty licks between my sediments—

burns at your touch now.
    How did you not hear me yell?

Why did you keep on
    when I started to flail?

If I weren't   already covered in scars,
    if your mxn didn't find these endearing

—bury themselves in the horror
    of my inescapable taxonomy—

would you have bowed your head to my bruised columns?
    Fed your mouth to any of my mouths?

Blow at my surface and wonder at my survival
    say: *however did you make it here?*

Was your lust for my obedience
　　always a lust for my terror?

Could you have loved me without my agony?
　　Without my fear? Have you not been paying attention?

All I wanted was to be held,
　　a willing servant of your desire;

To be your relief and your elucidation,
　　your patient remembering of release.

But animal—you have done your worst,
　　taken what wasn't yours to take and now

I am　　your death
　-defying　　　　　　lover.

I am a beacon of: I do whatever the fuck I want
　　and what I want now　　　　　　is to know

some things—heal; to unclench
　　the map of my evanescent unpropagated desire

from your careless ties.
　　What I want　　　　　　now

is for you to pull out
　　so I can rebuild what you've broken.

What I want now is　　to rub at myself
　　in long, unmitigated waves—

until you are forgotten
　　by my body.

I am prepared   above and beyond
        for the permanence of your exit.

I am heavy with it. I cannot blink
        and I cannot stop

the knowing of how
        we will   end.

ON BEING BURIED IN THE HAYS COUNTY JAIL

I only remember

what little was left of my words,
falling out of me into pale sheets
stapled and stiff. Meeting my maker
on a tiny tv screen. My chin tacked to
my chest, my lips stitched tight
and my body out of breath as they
misnamed me. A hungry thief
unfolding, exponentially, I was
a quiet but infinite scream
dressed in gallows of orange,
a pillar of smoke floating
from one hole to the next.
There, I was more than a fetish,
I was a recipe for nostalgia;
something savory and comforting
for the klan in the cold state of Texas;
nothing more than a roach
breeding in the ventricle,
infesting the gray muscle
of that pauper's house.
Soothing myself in the semi-dark,
I grafted my wounds with wool
and ink. Fractured by the hour.

I only remember

the feral way I dug down, looking
for a way out. Publicly acceptable
forms of suicide, any dignified version
of self-mutilation, any pithy metaphor
other womxn could learn from
when they read about my death
in the paper.

I daydreamed

about bridges and highway lanes
I could drift across, lift off and scatter.
Always on a sunny day. Always
on a weekend. Always
with a big, blue sky.

I dreamed

I swallowed gallons of saltwater down,
until I didn't have to anymore, until
my body relaxed and I stared at the bluest black;
until I sank among the bodies
of a thousand un-excavated pearls
that passively strangled
the pale, thin neck of the river.

I remember

how even as a gxrl, I had wondered
if I, too, would be forced to lay at the bottom.
A secret or a salt puddle beneath the city.
A spill of oil. Unseen and untouched and gone.

RELEASE||RELEASE

In the Hays County Jail, there is only one window
and it is the same size as the cheap, worn mystery
novel I pick up from the book cart on the third day.

> For weeks, I forget what the sun felt like.
> I forget I was once loved. I forget affection.
> I pray into a yellow legal pad. I pray into stupid
> Christian pamphlets. I pray into a steel bed.
> I pray into my one glass of pasteurized milk.
> I am still praying when I look up at the worn tv
> perpetually floating above our pod, to see a wolf's face
> leaping across the screen on channel 8. A vortex
> in the static, he dances, his body swiftly looping around
> something unmoving. I don't see what he is dancing around
> because I am crying at all the green on the ground.
> *When was the last time I had green?*

> That day, they take us, single file, out
> onto a half-court. Someone grabs the mostly dead
> basketball. Others start pacing around the box. I slip
> into poems, soothe myself by muttering
> rhythmic soliloquies. Old photos of myself
> fall out of my mouth and into my hands.

> When I am finally released, I make it
> as far as the gas station a half-a-block away
> before ripping stitch. I stand out in the open,
> suffocating, drowning
> in the Texas sun

> —a snake
> with no nest and no eggs
> and no good meat.

ASMR SLEEPCAST: THE NIGHT AFTER BEING RELEASED FROM THE RURAL COUNTY JAIL

for Sandra Bland

The highway swells like tide and I lie awake, willing
dozens of wheels to swerve loose of the pile-up
I know is coming, always comes, when I am away,
being Black and bothered. Under its waves, coyotes
make long-distance calls with the dog from the apartment
above me. All night, someone has been mad or lighting up
over something the dog has done. *The dog must drown*
and there it goes, off into the wilderness, alone.
Late into the foggy afternoon the next day, I listen
to the glass bottles and ash-cans roll softly down the sidewalk
of Aquarena Springs Drive, into uncut grass and trees
outlined in neon signals for shearing; into the wet and cluttered
clearing dotted with grocery bags and baby blankets,
tied up like walls and hanging from a few dozen branches.
The acetic origin of this low-rent luxury view is a parking lot by the river
filled with hundreds of kennels, and inside them: thousands of dogs
calling out to the woods. From my bed on the floor by the window,
I can faintly hear the drooling specters of Hays County: murmuring curses
over cards, their plastic chips swept roughly across coarse green felt;
their condoms unwrapped under restaurant tables;
the twist and spit of their Tampicos sweating;
the creaking yawn of their bar's wooden door left hanging on its hinge;
the quick lick of a flame brought to a small still-green   pasture
rolled tight and dank between their lips; and over it all—
the constant pulse of a siren circling my building—hungry;
yet another judge's thick-headed gavel trying to snap into place:
the cellophane, a dog, and someone's wheels.

Here, we can only ever fall asleep
to the sounds of the river flooding.

DO NOT CALL US BY OUR DEAD NAMES:
A DOCUPOEM

Chicago, Illinois | August 2019

> *Do not call us by our dead names!* my sister yells
> to the Border Patrol agent, her mouth knocked open,
> overrun with the smoke of lavender; a womxn
> under-loved, but alive, she exists—born running
> loose in the Chihuahuan Desert.

+

I go by she/her and I am from Guatemala.

+

She is a savant of transitions having come
across two Americas. Twice. She says,
the first time she came, she came
alone.

When they put me in the detention   they didn't know.
They put me   put me in.   I told them
I am a womxn—but they put me in   alone.
They said it was for safety—but I was alone for months.

The second time, they put me   with the men.
*   It was horrible.*

+

> And her name is a mirror of names flooding—
> prayers I receive hourly via inbox. An email
> from "Susana en La Ciudad" says:
>
> *La violencia—el feminicidio—me siguen*
> *sin cansarse, dentro y fuera de Juarez.*
> *Este humo sabe a fábrica. Ven aca, mijas!*

Nos vamos por la mañana!

The violence—the murdered women—they follow me
without getting tired, in and out of Juarez.
This smoke tastes like a factory. Come girls!
We're leaving in the morning!

It has only been seven days since
she sent the message *pero*
where she exists now,
no sé.

+

San Marcos, TX | March 2020

I am still *en la lucha!*
con mis hermanas porque

      my city is a river
of college students destined to be
      swallowed by the rural expanse
         of the Guadalupe.

En protesta, we comrades float
outside of the federal building,
    —the county jail where I was buried—
    En la lucha! against
the waves of the recently shipped,
    the waves of the soon to be drowned,
       and the waves of white faces swimming
happily in and out of the front doors.

In this war of mar y sol,
    we are all Largemouth Bass
       our tongues flipping back and forth
       between dos idiomas porque

　　　　　　　what happens to our people—
　　　happens to us.
What happens to us—
　　　happens to our people.
　　　　　　We are all still living
　　　at the intersection of:
　　　　　　　　　legal and barely legal.

　　　We are a festival
of the county's most wicked—
　　　dancing, drinking, and chanting
　　　　　　long after
　　　the music stops playing.

　　　+

Austin, TX | June 2020

A Texas Parks' infomercial explains that the Lavender Orchid Vine survives
　　　into the low twenties. It can recover—even if frozen to the ground.

This is all I needed to know, so I turn off the twenty-four-hour news coverage
　　　with its static videos of me

　　　and other indignant Black womxn from yesterday's rally,
　　　some in our twenties, pacing outside

of Governor Abbott's mansion, calling for parolees to be freed.
　　　At the rally, the large braids and straight backs of us

　　　Black womxn were bracketed by the fences
　　　　　　　of the capitol's manicured grounds;

our N95 masks, a dermis tagged
　　　in the nettled dialects of our dead.

Some of us wanted our husbands back
    —and not in body bags.

Others wanted to know: In how many ways could we be murdered
    before we were allowed to be galled?

    It was a familiar scene.
    There were mothers there—at the mansion.

But there are always mothers there,
    with their chins tucked, their chests shattering.

    And there are still mothers there,
    at the Pearsall Immigrant Detention Center

forty minutes away, shattering.
    In Austin—the people's heads floated

    over the photos of their children.
        In San Antonio—their heads still float

    over the heads of their children,
now fallen flat and frozen to the ground.

    +

        Half-asleep, I ask if the highway is a swallow
        of the unflowered—an inflorescence slivering through

        the meaty brown thigh of the Southwest,
        up the long Black neck of Houston,

        and down through the empty womb of Corpus Christi?
        I wonder, is it true? Has the highway always been a violence—
        a guillotine slowly severing us from our names?

AFTER BREONNA, I TRIED DATING AGAIN

for Breonna Taylor

The dirt of my skin   is peppered with dozens of dying stars.
My hands, over my head and tied to the eclipse
are becoming   as rank as old meat

from the locked-down market.   I do not love
what they've made of me. Every time I open my eyes
the swell of my shadow   surprises me.

I do not recognize   this bloated core or
these sagging nipples, rippling tight   back into my soft and ample.
I do not recognize   the dimpled back-half of me

or my crooked spine or my broken toes. I do not recognize
the stern brown blade over my eyes   or the chapped mouth
or the wagging elbows. In the mirror is an imposter, a liar.

Every morning, I ask What happened? Where am I? What happened? Who are you?
But whenever the imposter leans to answer a car hurdles out,
through a crowd of teeth, up and over the crease of their lips.

Indigo goes an eye, cardinal goes the other.   All I can hear
is a siren followed by a mother's tears   followed by a siren
followed by a father's tears   followed by   a siren   a siren   a siren.

Did you know   the once-warm soil of my skin would be enough
to grow a guillotine from?   Apart from my mouth, this beating
body, the heart of the year you were buried   is all that remains and barely.

Here is my mouth, love, stained. Syringe suck out
my lyric, the last of our memory in my chest—an epistle blue.
It is all that remains at the end of this decade.

Auxiliary were the sweaty and sun-choked
afternoons in which I made my cavernous silhouette
a swirl of sound and suck. There a kiss. Here   a medley.

But everywhere, everywhere where I knew you last.
Every morning, every shower   is a new eulogy in your name.
If my sex now were an affirmation it'd be: *No Peace. No Peace.*

How every Black death in the news reminds me
of the last time I was loved   without requirement.
I no longer love   to see my body

like a bruise on the mattress, like the only place
for their pain   is somewhere
rooted in me.   I have gained 95 pounds.

I gorged myself   on 87,600 hours' worth of news.
My chin is heavier now   with bullets pulled from dozens   of my sisters.
My loves—I am nothing like the Black womxn you once met by the water.

Swimming in my fat neck is the music of the deserted, their verve swift and sudden rushes
through the notches and nicks   of my cervix
while I sleep.   I go to the mirror   and she is not me and I am not her

and we are not ourselves. I cannot remember where I left myself.
I cannot remember   which pocket   I stored your ashes in.
I cannot find my candlesticks   or my lighter   or the stone that I came from.

I cannot remember   where I am supposed to be   right now—let alone
what it means to love   a pistol   emptied of its ammunition.

SELF-CARE

I begged the year for intimacy. Dashed down into my sheets
with nothing but the fan on. I begged my knees for oil, to bend
easy guillotine around some neck, maybe cut off the lamp in my belly,
knock out the dust from my toes, sweep out the tricks webbing up my corneas.
I said *give me back my wata* and the sleep number started seizing
—put a hump in the hour—but no more. When I finally gave up, I went
to the mirror for a look-see and found that *bitch* sucking face
with last winter when I'd come close to the Mojave's affection
only to float on too quick and too far West. Seeing me
she said *something I can do for you?* Shaking my head
I let her go on, got me some coffee and went back to work
feeding myself pretty lyrics and lead.

THE LITERAL CONTEXT FOR THE PHRASE "BANG! BANG!"

I.   *Definitions*

        Ballistics: What we think we know of these things.
        Ballad: An oral hallucination of our fanatic histories.
        Blame: A reasonable exit strategy for the iron-fisted.

II.   *Ballad*

        It is a dead thing in the poet's hands if it has no threat.

If it's without its teeth.
If it's without its grunge.
If it has no pulse.

III.   *Ballistics*

        We lug ammunition in our larynxes; language is

        our artillery's oxidization, at first utterance.
        Like a protestor's cell phone

        disconnecting in the police station
        and reconnecting outside

        of our country's deconstructed civility—
        poets are providing the network

        with the same alchemy used to conjure
        this nation up out of the colonies.

        We Americans were born from war,
        so to war do we turn

        and return.

IV.   *Ballad*

Every makeshift martyr, recently made

coughed up the delineated design
of a truly American death: starvation
for those found guilty of being human
and condemned for being less.

V.   *Blame*

These days hold
no respite for our children,
no sanctuary has been found.
We are still hunted—

in our schools, in our hospitals

in our kitchens, in our driveways
in our bedrooms, in our grocery stores
in our gardens, in our backyards
in our churches, in our community centers

—marooned are we Black womxn and mxn
by the "Everyman,"

(what he means is white man)
and his star-sick affections

for Order and Law, a sickly homage
to the so-called "sanctity

of things being destroyed:
our freedom of speech,
our freedom of movement,
our freedom of religion,"

and his freedom to gnash his teeth freely.

His free sees me docile
and kept; his free keeps us all
chewing on lead; us all afraid
to drive alone at night.

Hence the fire.

VI.   *Ballistics*

We seize *Amen!* with our lungs. So be the fire
that curdles in our compressed throats,
foams forever over the Black womxn's
bruised lips—a calligraphy of genuine love.

We hold *Hallelujah!* in our grasps; a yellow tape
slathered across the ghost of our dying radical.

Hallelujah! jangles against our sun-cloaked skins,
sweats down our knuckles, the melt of our bodies

a new constitution set
to drown the unfaithful
in their own acrid bile.

VII.   *Ballad*

There's no easy way to say that when I die, no one will remember
me, exactly as I was: an anxious Yes! For a change.

But a change of the caliber kind.

FOR THE SAKE OF MYSELF

I have no enemies and I have no friends
    —I have only this love for myself.

A love which is, at its root, a love for
    everyone who has made me myself—my kin.

Let us remember, love is the door to forgiveness
    but forgiveness is not permission

for other selves to separate me from myself.
    Nor is forgiveness permission to ignore

or allow the separation of other selves
    from themselves.

To take from me my body—my voice—
    is to steal from me, myself.

And I live for the sake of myself,
    for my own pleasure;

the metronome of my identity,
    a dense dimension floating between delightful states of being.

For the sake of myself, I forgive those I love,
    and I do love all of my other selves,

but should my other selves ever be tempted
    to take me from myself,

permit them to live,
    I might not.

MERCY

Mercy: to be released
from the limitations of others
with their dust-covered thresholds
and net-covered windows
to find myself naked
out in the mist-covered yard
picking dandelions for tea.

Mercy: to be considered·
when others craft their spells,
the geometric shape of my love
an impulsive element
throbbing relentlessly against their fear
from beneath the shadows
decorating the glass of their telescopes;
crawling steadily across the atlas
of their kitchen tables.

A LIBERATION ALL MY OWN

All I've ever wanted:

The hug and smile of a child buoyed
by their elder's dreams made real;

To be finally settled
in my grief;

The time and space
to unfurl, come undone;

The access to myself unencumbered
by the insecurity of a shelter-less road;

To fill four glowing walls
with pens, papers, books, and words;

To fill all the hours in between our righteous missives
with music, laughter, and dance;

To be trusted with my vision
and the patience it takes in practice;

To learn and be learned
in the fight for our lives;

To open a fridge
full;

To rest in a bed
warm;

To have a single dime
to my name;

To have my name
be held;

To watch the sun drown
every room in this house with its wonder;

To experience a liberation
all my own.

THE PURSUIT

"What are you waiting for?"

—Gabrielle Bouliane, from
"Don't You Dare Waste Your Fucking Time"

AFTER THE FESTIVAL

When I left behind
        || the festival ||
I became a wandering lust, a winding spark, distorted in the turn.

When I left behind
        || the dusty silhouette of my mother's tear-stained amen ||
                || her crushed eggshells circling the bed ||
I became a scattering of wishes left floating in the air.

When I left behind
        || the black smoke of my father's desert storm-soaked aurora ||
                || a thief slipping in through the cracked window||
I became Ogun returned from the war.

When I left behind
        || the globed fists of my sisters clutching white bread soaked through with honey ||
                ||little hungers sucking little joys out of little dreams||
I became Oshun's answer to little prayers.

When I left behind
        || the thin plastic frames of my bifocals tethered together with scotch tape ||
                ||a magnification turned from the sun to the ants in the grass||
I became an easy weapon when turned to the page.

When I left behind
        || the young evergreen teetering in the school yard I dreamed beneath alone ||
                ||the first of my ancestors to make themselves known||
I became a riot in Los Angeles.

When I left behind
        || the crumbling bridge of my body seizing on a playground's faded swing ||
                || a fist meant for my face penetrating my chest ||
I became a battleground for whispers.

When I left behind

|| the first of anyone's praying hands tangling my peach tule at the prom ||
||a taste of erotic pressure introduced to my mutating shape||
I became Erzulie in the dark.

When I left behind
|| the twinned flames of her and his hands snatching at the wet curls of my nape ||
||the slippery destination of anyone with a good enough reason||
I became Oyá—making shift happen.

When I left behind
|| the dozens of half-lit hallways flood with half-empty plastic red cups ||
||sleeping bags of bodies burned by my mischief||
I became Legba and I haven't stopped talkin' since.

When I left behind
|| the explosion of his wish welcoming mine ||
||my houngan lost to the drum||
I became Damballah, swinging eggs from my teeth.

When I left behind
|| the singular spotlight ceasing slow against the closing velvet of his last day alive ||
|| the silence of the theatre long after the crowd had left ||
I became this animal you see before you now.

I became a wandering lust
        yearning for the dimming
            delights of my innocence,
                for the borderless potential
                    of my desire to reign
                        over the whole
                                of my existence.

COSMIC DAWN

"Quantum mechanics allows two or more particles to exist in . . . an entangled state.
What happens to one of the particles in an entangled pair determines what happens
to the other particle, even if they are far apart."

—Press release for the Nobel Prize in Physics, October 4, 2022

A litany of frequencies rush along the obscure stretch
of my pliant continent; bursting gamma rays gone torrent,
in my hands they are a beginning. Once, I was a kind of dawn.
I evaded the foraging of my infinite bodies. I was unsiphoned
by the curiosity of men; the unsatiated desire of my species
seeking to possess my secrets left spinning out
in the known verse. I kept close the blued caulk rim
of my wet purse, a shimmering dust sanctioned
from coming loose. But I am, we are, the unwieldly
remnants of stars. We sprang from this compact planet feral,
radically free of any specific definition and naturally called
into the watery beds of our known histories
to fuse together our fragile bodies until we knocked nuclear.
I touch myself now and sense century after century
of solar adaptations flickering through the skirts
of a cold and boundless night. Fashioned by fire,
we could have been anything instead of obsessed
with breaking down and splitting. Too often we give into fear.
Succumb to the hunger of our own enigmatic flares,
distance ourselves from any imitation of an Other:
strange and unfamiliar, but we are all tethered—
why on Earth would we ever cede to borders?
In our blood, the helix spins. Same as this small planet spins.
All around us, the wheel, it turns. And still, we turn
away from our mirrors? Our bodies, like all other celestial bodies,
rotate endlessly from son to soil to sun. We know
that to ignore our entangled lives is to make each of us unreal,
our realities unrecognized, thus unrepaired and unsealed.
So I reach into the glowing swell of my own waist, an unmeasurable absence

warping the days and distances of our collective evolution,
to lose myself in my own inescapable gravity.
Wade the mutable circumstances of my bright blackness,
migrate its stretches of dark energy grown hefty, wide, and endless
in the sphere of this jaundiced kiln, inside myself, inside our selves,
to find some alternate version of healed, knowing that if I can come—
we can come together.

AT THE END OF TIME: IYA NI WURA, BABA NI JIGI

"Mother is gold, the father is a mirror."

—Oludamola Adebowale, from "Understanding the Cultural and Traditional
Importance of Mothers in Yorùbá Society"

I bow before my many names—
    The stratified prayer of my ancestors:
    iya ati baba mi, mi abuelo y abuela,
    m' uncail angus aintin, and all of my sleeping
    sisters or brothers.

I bow before my many names—
    my stiff tongue clinging to the roof
    of my mouth: a child without a teat.

I bow before my many names—
    and not their god. The same god
    who hurled his white-hot meteor
    into our emollient. A sergeant of sapphire
    still charging across our thresholds
    and into our womxn, evaporating
    in the fiery tear of yet another
    greedy night. The womxn vanished quick
    like tinseled marble eternally cut out
    from the breast of an eon or a She,
    a god of another name we have all forgotten.

I bow before my many names—
    the solemn gesture of an eroding topography.
    That I was once someone whole and am now
    an accent stuttering through an identity. That I am
    now an asteroid plummeting into the gaping mouths
    of Hir descendants branched out in the flushed indigo
    desert of here. That I am still a faith compressed

in his filtered memory of my existence's origin—
makes me sojourn.

I bow before my many names—
    a black descent into the expanse of earth's madness,
    swallowing whole rivers of light that rise in the void, slice through
    leaving scratches in the zodiac and on the lids of their eyes
    and making me a flake of Hir original form.

    Like a universe, unceremoniously unraveled
    in god's murderous light-stained hands, I am
    everything, anything, able to move—moved.

CRASH MOLASSES

in the mountains, we remove our clothes   those costume carcasses, charter atlas
rid ourselves of sorrow, its mediocrity   its hesitant ache, savants of the massifs

we erode, set fire to the broken   sands, hover beside them
catch, glory: the slow burn of it all   tetras of a lost moon, tearing into our chests

gravity sans kinetic   we have learned to climb out of each other
ruined cages, manifest: gods in us   all the confessions of our climax, allowed to atrophy

or expand   like the eviscerated land, with her fat highways
stretched, her blood-orange border   laced, hitched and heavy around her waist;

rivers

between the which ways; flooding hot and quick   between her rocky columns in our
ritual: the mock of the beginning   between the moonrise, the sun-slip

in hungering spaces   our bodies knock, cyclically
in sync with the other   unknown; crashing molasses

into stone, over the rim of the world   we move, from exit to existence
but always home, the spheres of our songs   harbor: heat

crawl back into our bodies heavy, singed   renegades, witnesses

QUANTUM LEAP

Waking, I stir beneath the soft warning
of another aubade slipping deep
into the moist soil of my   corporeal shape.
Beneath the glimmer of my bedsheets, I am
a dreaming animal dissatisfied with breath
alone. And I still want to ride the silhouette

    of earnest sleep
    until the world returns
    to green.

I wink and flash beneath the alchemy
of clear waters, crops and gardens grown arcane,
fish and fowl plenty, herds and hearts like mine
surviving this continent after a catastrophe of climate, thriving
in the many turns of time. These dreams bring me
to crest and shake and still in the mellow of my mattress.

Begging the air for my inertia, for my movements
unencumbered by fealty to any single shape or sound
or linear track of existence,
I stretch my thighs open to feel the ache of my sinew.
Grasping the pillow, I glance into the mirror
of these short fiery hours, and clutch

the pink clouds of my toes, the salmon rings
of my fingers, roll the meaty pirouette
in my mouth; canvas the warm dirt
of my biceps, graceful and fat,
swung open to greet the burn.
That I am alive, again,

after coming across every threshold of the year
—a universe exiting and entering my bed
with the casualness of a familiar yet dispassionate lover—

is my grace. I know my scent
will cling to the metal of my box springs,
my sweat a signature I'll leave for others to find:

I was human, imperfect and aging quick,
a single star falling amongst many
in the early summer of this century.

A MAP OF MY WANT

I.

My family drove from the clogged skylines of California
    to the gates of my father's Eden in Texas. His heaven—a continent's worth of dirt
        and dark potential: a heap of dead wood, dirt, snakes, rabbits, and dogs
            with gums that glittered pink in the face of silence.

+

I dreamed the road turned river and I floated as one
    of four spare tires in the backseat of my momma's whirring machine.
My momma hadn't liked my cousins teaching me to rotate
    my hips with my hands in California; round my back when bent over
        the stairs with my little nasty ass kicking like an engine in the air.
        Pop! Pop!

    She said *That's how*
                it happens.
                        That's how you become
                                a factory.

I have always been a burden of hours.
    The flesh-dense memory of my mother's ichor,
        I was always the language of lost time.
            A percolating wound driving through

                        some state or another in search of—

Asleep, I floated away
    from the shivering concrete
        of California, the state where I was
            originally manufactured in a city
                too strung out on murky neon and pasteurized prisoners.

Where thieves and killers and pot-smoking dogs
lived in cages tall and wide as state-owned buildings
downtown. Where I learned to load a magazine clip before I learned

to borrow sugar.

We left and I knew leaving meant
no cages for me but still—

I slept through
the first part of the drive.

II.

Once, I was a womxn.
Am now an arc, a memory

of exactly where my sisters sank
beneath the ruins of their former selves;
a cloud of unclasped bras and empty pockets;
our husked love entangled in the cottonwood branches
of the Chihuahuan Desert.

Excised in the open mouth
of the corrugated expanse,
we are the kind that live

in the closets
of the coyote willows.

+

From the edge, we surge north//northeast
listening to each other drip in the silence

of the land between; my sisters and I sliding up
against the tilted walls of the highway.

Like coins in the other's pockets
we are mutable shades

sharing values.

+

The more suns we swallow, the more sons try to swallow us.

+

Would you believe that my first
real conversation was with my soiled hands?

Me praying the landscape
of my irrigated memory?

Is how I know I am of the lake,
a dog of the ocean.

The sound of myself lapping
the lapping of myself—

in an unending ritual
of salutation and praise

for the tangible chaos
I wear like galaxies in the skin.

+

I was a womxn.
Am now an arc remembering

exactly where my sisters and I sank
beneath the ruins of ourselves—

the loam of our love, an unforgiving fatigue
freshly wet with the memories

of our first bodies, a cloudless mirror
filled with unclasped bras and empty pockets.

+

We surge through south\\southwest\\
                              /north//northeast/

                    listening to each other bleed
in the silence

                                        of the land
                                           in between.

+

I slept through
            the sound of the other factories
            I knew were being excised;

            Their steel frames uprooted and moved
            in the dark—into the open mouth
                        of the desert—their candy-soft frames
                        easily dying under the coyote willow.

            When I did finally wake, I was in a belly
            of blue yonder, my body gliding through
            the tall slate walls of Arizona's wide-hipped mountains

                        //

        I wasn't supposed to know—but I knew

THAT was what love felt like:

         a gape
in the noise of modern industry;

                                        an untested azure
                        thanking the petroleum that slides through it
                                    by holding it in its mouth—

                                before graciously swallowing;
                                love

                                is the sun's underestimated static
                        imbedding itself into my rib—
my melanin: a patchwork of time.

+

The only other kinds of factories
        that know what it is to be   excised

in the open mouth of the desert

are the kind that live under the coyote willow.
The kind   that will eat out a poem

                        before they are dragged back
                            into a snake pit.

III.

                                Sometimes, they put the detention centers
                                far back from the highway

                                                in the back

                                        like the eggs in Walmart
                                        they want you to buy

          everything
          but the land.

          Float by
                              without being
                                        disturbed.

IV.

The first boi I feel anything for kisses my sister under a lemon tree.
The next boi I feel anything for kisses me on the cheek, never walks me home again.
The next boi I feel anything for vomits on my shoes and never says my name again.
The next boi I feel anything for   again.
The next   feel   for   home

                    falls, laughing, through my front door.
                         Takes me to twilight, a glass sky
                              stained lavender. The boi
                         tapes a skateboard
                                                  to my feet
                                                       and I

          glide.

V.

To my father, we—I am, an endemic of love.

The day's heat—my love.
The bark scorpion—my love.
The gap between the borders—our love.

               We—I am
               more than this love.

91

A saguaro of love.

Whatever my mother/father could have been—it lives in us-me.
I have got the burden of them both in my body. We were born like this.

A glaze of unbiased binaries.
A crocheted concoction of womxn.
Pulling on   whatever it was he/she was   before us.

A breed of immaculate violence   a womxn evaporating
in the swell of yet another of this country's greedy nights.

We—I am
the child of a dog:

the progeny of a monsoon:
a fetish of unadulterated light and cystic hunger.

The uncut sky
sick with onyx.

But I never wanted to know that to be a womxn is to always be
heavy with someone else's suns.

VI.
Those sons under my suns underestimated my evolutionary hunger.

I bite back. I arc and sift.
More or less, I am

what it is
to be

known.

ACKNOWLEDGMENTS

This second collection of poems was directly supported and uplifted by the follow-ing organizations and institutions: Right of Return USA at The Center for Art and Advocacy, Tin House, Black Mountain Institute, Civil Rights Corps, Sierra Nevada University, Detention Watch Network, Texas After Violence Project, and the Art for Justice Fund. Thank you for affording me the time and space to rest, restore, and dream.

Ample gratitude and praise to the individuals whose kind words, time, and moral support encouraged me during the development of this book: Troy Baham Jr., Tamara Bates, Sara Ortiz, Deborah D.E.E.P. Mouton, Mary South, Murphy Anne Carter, Chib-bi Orduña, Candyce Tuggle, Billy Tuggle, Carmendy Tuggle, Shaneen Harris, and my sister Katonya Hicks. Each of you shine so brightly in my heart.

To my agent Annie Hwang, I thank you for having faith in my work, sticking with me, and for helping me find the best home for my work. To my editor Maya Marshall, this book would not have been possible without you. Thank you for making space for me to be my whole self!

To Gretchen Bouliane, beyond the words and love of Gabrielle, it has been your continued love and support that made it important for me to include Gabby in this col-lection. After all these years, she continues to inspire me and I know that is because of you and yours. Thank you for bringing such a wonderful person into the world.

Special thanks to the editors and readers of the following publications, in which early versions of these poems first appeared:

Academy of American Poets, Poem-A-Day: "Self-Care"

Adroit Journal: "Steel Horses"

American Poetry Review: "The Skybridge in Their Divorce," "Bonfire Brides," "For-eign Bodies," "BDSM: Before Dusk, Say Maybe," "At the End of Time: Iya Ni Wura, Baba Ni Jigi"

F(r)iction Lit: "After the Widow and I Compare Funerals," "Quantum Leap"

Frontier Poetry: "On Becoming a Bridge for the Binary" (Originally published as "Arco")

Hayden's Ferry Review: "Chiron's Breach"

Kweli Journal: "Crash Molasses"

Northwest Review: "A Map of My Want"

Scalawag: "A Tale as Old as Time"

Split This Rock: "After the George Floyd Protests, My Strange Dream"

Sundog Lit: "#LoveMachine"

Torch Literary Arts: "The Literal Context for the Phrase 'Bang! Bang!,'" "On Being Buried in the Hays County Jail"

Yale Review: "ASMR Sleepcast: The Night After Being Released from the Hays County Jail"

The poem "I Tried Dating Again" was chosen by Victoria Chang as the winner of *Palette Poetry*'s 2020 Sappho Award.

The poem "A Liberation All My Own" was selected and displayed by curator Daisy Desrosiers for the Art for Justice Fund's 2023 "No Justice Without Love" Exhibition in the Ford Foundation Gallery.

ABOUT THE AUTHOR

Faylita Hicks (she/they) is a queer Afro-Latinx writer, multidisciplinary artivist, and cultural strategist who integrates transformative justice theory into their creative practice, using much of their work to advocate for the lives of marginalized people in our global majority. Their personal account of pretrial incarceration in Hays County is featured in the ITVS Independent Lens 2019 documentary "45 Days in a Texas Jail," and the Brave New Films 2021 documentary narrated by Mahershala Ali, "Racially Charged: America's Misdemeanor Problem."

Newly based in Chicago, Illinois, Hicks is a voting member of the Recording Academy/GRAMMYs and its Songwriters and Composers Committee, and the author of the critically-acclaimed debut poetry collection *HoodWitch* (Acre Books, 2019), a finalist for the 2020 Lambda Literary Award for Bisexual Poetry, the 2019 Julie Suk Award, and the 2019 Balcones Poetry Prize. Their memoir, *A Body of Wild Light*, is forthcoming from Haymarket Books.

ABOUT HAYMARKET BOOKS

Haymarket Books is a radical, independent, nonprofit book publisher based in Chicago. Our mission is to publish books that contribute to struggles for social and economic justice. We strive to make our books a vibrant and organic part of social movements and the education and development of a critical, engaged, and internationalist left.

We take inspiration and courage from our namesakes, the Haymarket Martyrs, who gave their lives fighting for a better world. Their 1886 struggle for the eight-hour day—which gave us May Day, the international workers' holiday—reminds workers around the world that ordinary people can organize and struggle for their own liberation. These struggles—against oppression, exploitation, environmental devastation, and war—continue today across the globe.

Since our founding in 2001, Haymarket has published more than nine hundred titles. Radically independent, we seek to drive a wedge into the risk-averse world of corporate book publishing. Our authors include Angela Y. Davis, Arundhati Roy, Keeanga-Yamahtta Taylor, Eve L. Ewing, Aja Monet, Mariame Kaba, Naomi Klein, Rebecca Solnit, Olúfẹ́mi O. Táíwò, Mohammed El-Kurd, José Olivarez, Noam Chomsky, Winona LaDuke, Robyn Maynard, Leanne Betasamosake Simpson, Howard Zinn, Mike Davis, Marc Lamont Hill, Dave Zirin, Astra Taylor, and Amy Goodman, among many other leading writers of our time. We are also the trade publishers of the acclaimed Historical Materialism Book Series.

Haymarket also manages a vibrant community organizing and event space in Chicago, Haymarket House, the popular Haymarket Books Live event series and podcast, and the annual Socialism Conference.

ALSO AVAILABLE FROM HAYMARKET BOOKS

American Inmate
Justin Rovillos Monson

Before the Next Bomb Drops: Rising Up from Brooklyn to Palestine
Remi Kanazi

Black Queer Hoe
Britteney Black Rose Kapri, foreword by Danez Smith

DEAR GOD. DEAR BONES. DEAR YELLOW.
Noor Hindi

Light in Gaza: Writings Born of Fire
Edited by Jehad Abusalim, Jennifer Bing, and Mike Merryman-Lotze

The Limitless Heart: New and Selected Poems (1997–2022)
Cheryl Boyce-Taylor

Nazar Boy
Tarik Dobbs

O Body
Dan "Sully" Sullivan

Rifqa
Mohammed El-Kurd, foreword by aja monet

There Are Trans People Here
H. Melt